POSTCOLONIAL LOVE POEM

Also by Natalie Diaz

When My Brother Was an Aztec

POSTCOLONIAL LOVE POEM

NATALIE DIAZ

Graywolf Press

This publication is made possible, in part, by the voters of Minnesota through a Minnesota State Arts Board Operating Support grant, thanks to a legislative appropriation from the arts and cultural heritage fund. Significant support has also been provided by the McKnight Foundation, Target, the Lannan Foundation, the Amazon Literary Partnership, and other generous contributions from foundations, corporations, and individuals. To these organizations and individuals we offer our heartfelt thanks.

Published by Graywolf Press
250 Third Avenue North, Suite 600
Minneapolis, Minnesota 55401

www.graywolfpress.org

Published in the United States of America

ISBN 978-1-64445-014-7

8 10 11 9 7

Library of Congress Control Number: 2019933473

Cover design: Mary Austin Speaker

Cover photos: Natalie Diaz

Contents

←

I am singing a song that can only be born
after losing a country.

JOY HARJO

Postcolonial Love Poem

I've been taught bloodstones can cure a snakebite,
can stop the bleeding—most people forgot this
when the war ended. The war ended
depending on which war you mean: those we started,
before those, millennia ago and onward,
those which started me, which I lost and won—
these ever-blooming wounds.
I was built by wage. So I wage love and worse—
always another campaign to march across
a desert night for the cannon flash of your pale skin
settling in a silver lagoon of smoke at your breast.
I dismount my dark horse, bend to you there, deliver you
the hard pull of all my thirsts—
I learned *Drink* in a country of drought.
We pleasure to hurt, leave marks
the size of stones—each a cabochon polished
by our mouths. I, your lapidary, your lapidary wheel
turning—green mottled red—
the jaspers of our desires.
There are wildflowers in my desert
which take up to twenty years to bloom.
The seeds sleep like geodes beneath hot feldspar sand
until a flash flood bolts the arroyo, lifting them
in its copper current, opens them with memory—
they remember what their god whispered
into their ribs: *Wake up and ache for your life.*
Where your hands have been are diamonds
on my shoulders, down my back, thighs—
I am your culebra.
I am in the dirt for you.
Your hips are quartz-light and dangerous,
two rose-horned rams ascending a soft desert wash
before the November sky untethers a hundred-year flood—
the desert returned suddenly to its ancient sea.
Arise the wild heliotrope, scorpion weed,

blue phacelia which hold purple the way a throat can hold
the shape of any great hand—
Great hands is what she called mine.
The rain will eventually come, or not.
Until then, we touch our bodies like wounds—
the war never ended and somehow begins again.

We admitted that we were human beings
and melted for love in this desert.

MAHMOUD DARWISH

Blood-Light

My brother has a knife in his hand.
He has decided to stab my father.

This could be a story from the Bible,
if it wasn't already a story about stars.

I weep alacranes—the scorpions clatter
to the floor like yellow metallic scissors.

They land upside down on their backs and eyes,
but writhe and flip to their segmented bellies.

My brother has forgotten to wear shoes again.
My scorpions circle him, whip at his heels.

In them is what stings in me—
it brings my brother to the ground.

He rises, still holding the knife.
My father ran out of the house,

down the street, crying like a lamplighter—
but nobody turned their lights on. It is dark.

The only light left is in the scorpions—
there is a small light left in the knife too.

My brother now wants to give me the knife.
Some might say, *My brother wants to stab me.*

He tries to pass it to me—like it is a good thing.
Like, *Don't you want a little light in your belly?*

Like the way Orion and Scorpius—
across all that black night—pass the sun.

My brother loosens his mouth—
between his teeth, throbbing red Antares.

One way to open a body to the stars, with a knife.
One way to love a sister, help her bleed light.

These Hands, If Not Gods

Haven't they moved like rivers—
like glory, like light—
over the seven days of your body?

And wasn't that good?
Them at your hips—

isn't this what God felt when he pressed together
the first Beloved: *Everything*.
Fever. Vapor. Atman. Pulsus.
Finally, a sin worth hurting for, a fervor,
a sweet—*You are mine*.

It is hard not to have faith in this:
from the blue-brown clay of night
these two potters crushed and smoothed you
into being—grind, then curve—built your form up—

atlas of bone, fields of muscle,
one breast a fig tree, the other a nightingale,
both morning and evening.

O, the beautiful making they do,
of trigger and carve, suffering and stars.

Aren't they, too, the carpenters
of your small church? Have they not burned
on the altar of your belly, eaten the bread
of your thighs, broke you to wine, to ichor,
to nectareous feast?

Haven't they riveted your wrists, haven't they
had you at your knees?

And when these hands touched your throat,
showed you how to take the apple *and* the rib,
how to slip a thumb into your mouth and taste it all,
didn't you sing out their ninety-nine names—

Zahir, Aleph, hands-times-seven,
Sphinx, Leonids, locomotura,
Rubidium, August, and September—
and when you cried out, *O, Prometheans,*
didn't they bring fire?

These hands, if not gods, then why
when you have come to me, and I have returned you
to that from which you came—white mud, mica, mineral, salt—
why then do you whisper, *O, my Hecatonchire. My Centimani.*
My Hundred-Handed One?

Catching Copper

My brothers have
a bullet.

They keep their bullet
on a leash shiny
as a whip of blood.

My brothers walk their bullet
with a limp—a clipped
hip bone.

My brothers' bullet
is a math-head, is all geometry,
from a distance is just a bee
and its sting. Like a bee—
you should see my brothers' bullet
make a comb, by chewing holes
in what is sweet.

My brothers lose
their bullet all the time—
when their bullet takes off on them,
their bullet leaves a hole.

My brothers search their houses,
their bodies for their bullet,
and a little red ghost moans.

Eventually, my brothers call out,
Here, bullet, here—
their bullet comes running, buzzing.
Their bullet always comes
back to them. When their bullet comes
back to them, their bullet
leaves a hole.

My brothers are too slow
for their bullet
because their bullet is in a hurry
and wants to get the lead out.

My brothers' bullet is dressed
for a red carpet
in a copper jacket.
My brothers tell their bullet,
*Careful you don't hurt somebody
with all that flash.*

My brothers kiss their bullet
in a dark cul-de-sac, in front
of the corner-store ice machine,
in the passenger seat of their car,
on a strobe-lighted dance floor.
My brothers' bullet
kisses them back.

My brothers break and dance
for their bullet—the jerk,
the stanky leg. They pop, lock
and drop for their bullet,
a move that has them writhing
on the ground.
The worm, my brothers call it.
My brothers go all-worm
for their bullet.

My brothers' bullet is registered,
is a bullet of letters—has a PD,
a CIB, a GSW, if they are lucky
an EMT, if not, a Triple 9, a DNR,
a DOA.

My brothers never call the cops
on their bullet and instead pledge
allegiance to their bullet
with hands over their hearts
and stomachs and throats.

My brothers say they would die
for their bullet. If my brothers die,
their bullet would be lost.
If my brothers die,
there's no bullet to begin with—
the bullet is for living brothers.

My brothers feed their bullet
the way the bulls fed Zeus—
burning, on a pyre, their own
thigh bones wrapped in fat.
My brothers take a knee, bow
against the asphalt, prostrate
on the concrete for their bullet.

We wouldn't go so far
as to call our bullet
a prophet, my brothers say.
But my brothers' bullet
is always lit like a night-church.
It makes my brothers holy.

You could say my brothers' bullet
cleans them—the way red ants
wash the empty white bowl
of a dead coyote's eye socket.
Yes, my brothers' bullet
cleans them, makes them
ready for God.

From the Desire Field

I don't call it *sleep* anymore.
      I'll risk losing something new instead—

like you lost your rosen moon, shook it loose.

But sometimes when I get my horns in a thing—
a wonder, a grief, or a line of her—it is a sticky and ruined
      fruit to unfasten from,

despite my trembling.

Let me call my anxiety, *desire*, then.
Let me call it, *a garden*.

Maybe this is what Lorca meant
      when he said, *verde que te quiero verde*—

because when the shade of night comes,
I am a field of it, of any worry ready to flower in my chest.

My mind in the dark is una bestia, unfocused,
      hot. And if not yoked to exhaustion

beneath the hip and plow of my lover,
then I am another night wandering the desire field—

bewildered in its low green glow,

belling the meadow between midnight and morning.
Insomnia is like spring that way—surprising
      and many petaled,

the kick and leap of gold grasshoppers at my brow.

I am struck in the witched hours of want—

I want her green life. Her inside me
in a green hour I can't stop.
      Green vein in her throat green wing in my mouth

green thorn in my eye. I want her like a river goes, bending.
Green moving green, moving.

Fast as that, this is how it happens—
      soy una sonámbula.

And even though you said today you felt better,
and it is so late in this poem, is it okay to be clear,
      to say, *I don't feel good*,

to ask you to tell me a story
about the sweetgrass you planted—and tell it again
      or again—

until I can smell its sweet smoke,
      leave this thrashed field, and be smooth.

Manhattan Is a Lenape Word

It is December and we must be brave.

The ambulance's rose of light
blooming against the window.
Its single siren-cry: *Help me.*
A silk-red shadow unbolting like water
through the orchard of her thigh.

Her, come—in the green night, a lion.
I sleep her bees with my mouth of smoke,
dip honey with my hands stung sweet
on the darksome hive.
Out of the eater I eat. Meaning,
She is mine, colony.

The things I know aren't easy:
I'm the only Native American
on the 8th floor of this hotel or any,
looking out any window
of a turn-of-the-century building
in Manhattan.

Manhattan is a Lenape word.
Even a watch must be wound.
How can a century or a heart turn
if nobody asks, *Where have all
the Natives gone?*

If you are where you are, then where
are those who are not here? Not here.
Which is why in this city I have
many lovers. All my loves
are reparations loves.

What is loneliness if not unimaginable
light and measured in lumens—
an electric bill which must be paid,
a taxi cab floating across three lanes
with its lamp lit, gold in wanting.
At 2 a.m. everyone in New York City
is empty and asking for someone.

Again, the siren's same wide note:
Help me. Meaning, *I have a gift
and it is my body*, made two-handed
of gods and bronze.

She says, *You make me feel
like lightning.* I say, *I don't ever
want to make you feel that white.*
It's too late—I can't stop seeing
her bones. I'm counting the carpals,
metacarpals of her hand inside me.

One bone, the lunate bone, is named
for its crescent outline. Lunatus. Luna.
Some nights she rises like that in me,
like trouble—a slow luminous flux.

The streetlamp beckons the lonely
coyote wandering West 29th Street
by offering its long wrist of light.
The coyote answers by lifting its head
and crying stars.

Somewhere far from New York City,
an American drone finds then loves
a body—the radiant nectar it seeks
through great darkness—makes
a candle-hour of it, and burns
gently along it, like American touch,
an unbearable heat.

The siren song returns in me,
I sing it across her throat: *Am I
what I love? Is this the glittering world
I've been begging for?*

American Arithmetic

Native Americans make up less than
1 percent of the population of America.
0.8 percent of 100 percent.

O, mine efficient country.

I do not remember the days before America—
I do not remember the days when we were all here.

Police kill Native Americans more
than any other race. *Race* is a funny word.
Race implies someone will win,
implies, *I have as good a chance of winning as—*

Who wins the race that isn't a race?

Native Americans make up 1.9 percent of all
police killings, higher per capita than any race—

sometimes *race* means *run.*

I'm not good at math—can you blame me?
I've had an American education.

We are Americans, and we are less than 1 percent
of Americans. We do a better job of dying
by police than we do existing.

When we are dying, who should we call?
The police? Or our senator?
Please, someone, call my mother.

At the National Museum of the American Indian,
68 percent of the collection is from the United States.
I am doing my best to not become a museum
of myself. I am doing my best to breathe in and out.

I am begging: *Let me be lonely but not invisible.*

But in an American room of one hundred people,
I am Native American—less than one, less than
whole—I am less than myself. Only a fraction
of a body, let's say, *I am only a hand—*

and when I slip it beneath the shirt of my lover
I disappear completely.

They Don't Love You Like I Love You

My mother said this to me
long before Beyoncé lifted the lyrics
from the Yeah Yeah Yeahs,

and what my mother meant by,
Don't stray, was that she knew
all about it—the way it feels to need

someone to love you, someone
not *your kind*, someone white,
some one some many who live

because so many of mine
have not, and further, live on top of
those of ours who don't.

I'll say, say, say,
I'll say, say, say,
What is the United States if not a clot

of clouds? If not spilled milk? Or blood?
If not the place we once were
in the millions? America is "Maps"—

Maps are ghosts: white and
layered with people and places I see through.
My mother has always known best,

knew that I'd been begging for them,
to lay my face against their white
laps, to be held in something more

than the loud light of their projectors,
as they flicker themselves—sepia
or blue—all over my body.

All this time,
I thought my mother said, *Wait,*
as in, *Give them a little more time*

to know your worth,
when really, she said, *Weight,*
meaning *heft,* preparing me

for the yoke of myself,
the beast of my country's burdens,
which is less worse than

my country's plow. Yes,
when my mother said,
They don't love you like I love you,

she meant,
Natalie, that doesn't mean
you aren't good.

Skin-Light

My whole life I have obeyed it—:

    its every hunting. I move beneath it
    as a jaguar moves, in the dark
        liquid blading of shoulder.

The opened-gold field and glide of the hand,

    light-fruited and scythe-lit.

I have arrived to this god-made place—:

    Teotlachco, the ball court—:
    because the light called: *lightwards!*
        and dwells here: Lamp-Land.

    We touch the ball of light
    to one another—: split bodies, desire-knocked
        and stroked bright.
            Light reshapes my lover's elbow,

    a brass whistle.

I put my mouth there—: mercy-luxed, and come we both

    to light. It streams me.
    A rush of scorpions—:
        fast-light. A lash of breath—:
            god-maker.

    Light horizons her hip—: springs an ocelot
    cut of chalcedony and magnetite.
        Hip, limestone and cliffed,

slopes like light into her thigh—: light-box, skin-bound.

Wind shakes the calabash,
disrupts the light to ripple—: light-struck,
        then scatter.

This is the war I was born toward, her skin,

        its lake-glint. I desire—: I thirst.
        To be filled—: light-well.

The light throbs everything, and songs

        against her body, girdling the knee bone.
        Our bodies—: light-harnessed, light-thrashed.
                The bruising—: violet, bilirubin
                        bloom.

A work of all good yokes—: blood-light—:

        to make us think the pain is ours to keep,
        light-trapped, lanterned.
                That I asked for it. That I own it—:
                        lightmonger.

I am light now, or on the side of light—:

        light-head, light-trophied.
        Light-wracked and light-gone.

        The sweet maize in fluorescence—: an eruption
        of light, or its feast,
                from the stalk
                        of my lover's throat.

And I, light-eater, light-loving.

Run'n'Gun

I learned to play ball on the rez, on outdoor courts where the sky was our ceiling. Only a tribal kid's shot has an arc made of sky. We balled in the rez park against a tagged backboard with a chain for a net, where I watched a Hualapai boy from Peach Springs dunk the ball in a pair of flip-flops and slip on the slick concrete to land on his wrist. His radius fractured and ripped up through his skin like a tusk, which didn't stop him from pumping his other still-beautiful arm into the air and yelling, *Yeah, Clyde the Glide, motherfuckers!* before some adult sped him off to the emergency room.

I ran games in the abandoned school yard with an eight-foot fence we had to hop, where I tore so many pairs of shorts on the top spikes, and where when my little brother got snagged trying to climb down, my cousin and I let him hang by the waistband of his underwear for an entire game of eleven. And if that cousin hadn't overdosed on heroin a few years later, he might have proved us right and been the first rez Jump Man.

I got run by my older brother on our slanted driveway, the same brother I write about now, who taught me that there is nothing easy in our desert, who blocked every shot I ever took against him until I was about twelve years old. By then, his addictions had stolen his game, while I found mine.

I learned the game with my brothers and cousins, with my friends and enemies. We had jacked-up shoes and mismatched socks. Our knees were scabbed and we licked our lips chapped. We were small, but we learned to play big enough to beat the bigger, older white kids at the rec center on "The Hill," which to get to we crossed underneath the I-40 freeway, across the train tracks, and through a big sandy wash.

We played bigger and bigger until we began winning. And we won by doing what all Indians before us had done against their bigger, whiter opponents—we became coyotes and rivers, and we ran faster than their fancy kicks could, up and down the court, game after game. We became the weather—we blew by them, we rained buckets, we lit up the gym with our moves.

We learned something more important than fist, at least at that age. We learned to make guns of our hands, and we pulled the trigger on jumpers all damn day. And when they talked about the way we played, they called it, *Run'n'gun*, and it made them tired before they ever stepped on the court. Just thinking about a pickup game against us made the white boys from the junior high and high school teams go to sleep. While they slept, we played our dreams.

My country needs me, and if I were not here,
I would have to be invented.

HORTENSE SPILLERS

Asterion's Lament

You curving—you rivering and full—

     how did Theseus find no joy in you?

Let me be your tender captain, ferry

the ultramarine thread you unraveled

from your skein—to lead the most lost through

the labyrinth of your body.

     Go forward, always down, you said.

I know another name for *holy* is *water*—

I have suffered the hot hurt of thirst.

Only the mouthless would not anoint themselves

with your mouth, descend the violet-green

zigzagging the shoal of your collarbone,

hull their chests and fall upon your shore.

     I am alive, and coursing to drink

on the current of jet flowing sternum to nipple—

barefooted, slipped from my shirt, dizzy

for the silvered-green ribbons swimming

your wrists. How each flickered stream spills

into the agate cups of your palms. I will sink

the deep channel bending the sandhills

of your hips, down the jetties of your thighs.

In your hands I am a coming vessel,

an empty boat, willing to be helmsman or helmed,

moored, made fast—shackled and filled.

More pilgrimage than wandering. More mercy

than amaze. I will follow this wet map of you

along whatever remains of the corridors of my life.

And if you can close your eyes to the Minotaur

in me, with her heavy twist of horns, I can find you.

Go forward, always down, we will,

to the beauty and slake of a monster's appetite.

Like Church

My lover comes to me like darkfall—long,

and through my open window. Mullion, transom.

A good window lets the outside participate.

I keep time on the hematite clocks of her shoulders.

And I've done so much of it—*time*. Her right hip

bone is a searchlight, sweeping me, finds me.

I've only ever escaped through her body. What if

we stopped saying *whiteness* so it meant *anything*.

For example, if you mean milk of magnesia say

milk of magnesia, or *snow*, or they've hurt another

one of us, or the quarter moon is smoke

atop the dirty water, or the pearline damp she laces

up my throat, my face. *Mi caracol.* They think

brown people fuck better when we are sad.

Like horses. Or coyotes. All hoof or howl. All

mouth clamped down in the hair, on the neck,

slicked with latherin. You ask, *Who is they?*

even though you know. You want me to name

names. Shoot, we are named after them. You think

my Creator had heard of the word *Natalie*? Ha!

When he first made me he called me *Snake*—

then promised the afterlife would be reversed,

south turned north, full with tight bright melons.

Pluck one melon and another melon grows

in its place. But it's hard, isn't it? Not to perform

what they say about our sadness, when we are

always so sad. It is real work to not perform

a fable. Ask the turtle. Ask the hare. Remind

yourself and your friends: *Sometimes I feel fast.*

Sometimes I am so slow. Sometimes I get put down

in the street. Forever I win the wound they hang

on my chest. Remind yourself, your friends.

They are only light because we are dark.

If we didn't exist, it wouldn't be long before

they had to invent us. Like the light switch.

Yes, our Creator says *Kingdom* and we come.

Remind our friends. We fuck like we church—

best. And full of God, and joy, and sins, and

sweet upside-down cake. And when they ask me,

What's in your love's eyes? I tell them. Wild sugar-

melons, green-on-green, on green. She and I,

we eat the melons, starting at their thick-syruped

hearts, hold the beady seeds in our mouths

like new eyes, wait for them to leap open

and see us first.

Wolf OR-7

*When he left his pack to find a mate, Oregon's seventh
collared wolf, named OR-7 by state biologists, became
the first wolf in California since 1927, when the last one
was killed for government bounty.*

On a digital map, OR-7's trek is charted—by a GPS
tracking collar and numerous trail cameras—a trembling blue line,

south, west, south again,
twelve hundred miles from Oregon to California

to find *Her: gray wolf, Canis lupus, Loba, Beloved.*

In the tourmaline dusk I go a same wilding path,
pulled by night's map into the forests and dunes of your hips,

divining from you rivers, then crossing them—
proving the long thirst I'd wander to be sated by you.

I confuse instinct for desire—isn't *bite* also *touch*?

Some things cannot be charted—
the middle-night cosmography of your moving hands,

the constellation holding the gods
of your jaw and ear.

You tell me you take wolf naps, and I turn lupanar.

A female gray wolf's shoulders are narrower than a male's,
but our mythos of shoulders began before I knew that,

when I broke open my mouth upon yours

as we pressed against the glass doors of the cliff house
looking out into the bay's shadows hammering

the bronzed bell of the super moon.

My mind climbed the rise, fall, rise of your bared back.
In me a pack of wolves appeared and disappeared

over the hill of my heart.

I, too, follow toward where I am forever returning—
Her.

And somewhere in the dark
of a remote night-vision camera,

the quivering green music of animals.

Ink-Light

We move within the snow-chromed world: Like-animal. Like-deer. An alphabet. Along a street white as lamplight into the winter, walking—: like language, a new text. I touch her with the eyes of my skin.

The way I read any beloved—: from the ramus of the left jaw down to the cuneiform of the right foot. She isn't so much what she is—: and becomes herself only when added to the space where she isn't. What is touch—: not the touch not the hand but the white heat it floats through.

I count her my desires, mark her—: hoofprints across the frozen page. *Four strokes of dusk. Carbon black, Lamp black, Bone black, Hide glue*—: I am the alchemist of ink. She answers me, *Quicksilver,*

and the noise of her boots upon the snow is the weight of a night bird bending the meteor-blue branch fruiting white flames of cotton. Each of her steps, an allograph—: bird, flexed limb, perfect line of vertebrae, the glyph of my pelvis.

When I put my teeth to her wrist, the world goes everywhere white. Not sound but the dizzying nautilus of what is both the palm and the ear. I invented her hand in this texture—: a grapheme.

In me, a feeling—: white blossom with a red-sided icosahedron inside the velveteen car of a gold train vibrating the violet tunnel of my throat on its way to a dimmed station in my chest—: twenty seats of desire, and I am sitting in each one.

I burn on the silver sparks of her breath moving out of her body. The miracle. No. The power and the glory glory glory of her—: she breathes. Out—: Out—: twenty red seats of desire, I break every one. A series of waves against hammer anvil stirrup—: a vibration of light I can hold with my mouth.

The Mustangs

In another life, my older brother was a beautiful, muscular boy who could jump from a standing position to grab a missed shot right from the rim and either hit a waiting outlet on a fast break or spring back up and drop it through the net for an easy two points. He had thin ankles, long lean legs with high calf muscles balled tight like fists and split like upside-down hearts—runner's legs, jumper's legs, Indian legs. He also had the upper body of a Mojave man—wide-chested, broad-shouldered, arms and hands that hung down near his knees, *like slingshots* is what my mother says, meaning, *he is a fighter.*

He played varsity basketball for our small town high school, the Needles Mustangs. They wore royal blue and white. A bright blue mustang was painted on the front of the gymnasium, another inside against the brick wall, and a third in a circle on the wooden middle half-court. Mustangs. I associate them with basketball. I have felt them in me—hooves rumbling like weather in my ears and sternum, jolts of muscle like bolts in my throat—the way my brother must have felt those herds stampeding his veins in those years, and done his best to break them.

I love my brother best in memories such as this one: I sat in the rattling bleachers of the Needles Mustangs gymnasium with my mother, my father, and all of my siblings, watching my brother run out to the warm-up song "Thunderstruck" by AC/DC. It begins with an unhinged, chant-like yell, followed by the strike of the word *thunder* and then *thunderstruck*. The word *thunder* is growled fifteen times followed by nineteen war-cried versions of *thunderstruck*.

Dressed in Mustang-blue tear-away warm-up pants and shirts, my brother and his teammates—some of whom were from our reservation—were all glide and finesse. Their high tops barely touched the floor. They circled the court twice before crossing it and moving into a layup drill while "Thunderstruck" filled the gymnasium. They were all the things they could ever be—they were young kings and conquerors.

To that song, they made layup after layup, passed the ball like a planet be-tween them, pulled it back and forth from the floor to their hands like Mars. "Thunderstruck" played so loudly that I couldn't hear what my mother hollered to cheer my brother—I could only see her mouth opening and closing. I was ten years old and realized right there on those bleachers thundering like guns that this game had the power to quiet what seemed so loud in us—that it might have the power to set the fantastic beasts trampling our hearts loose. I saw it in my mother, in my brother, in those wild boys. We ran up and down the length of our lives, all of us, lit by the lights of the gym, toward freedom—we Mustangs. On those nights, we were forgiven for all we would ever do wrong.

Ode to the Beloved's Hips

Bells are they—shaped on the 8th day, silvered
percussion in the morning—*are* the morning.
Swing switch sway. Hold the day away a little
longer, a little slower, a little *easy*. Call to me—
*I wanna rock, I-I wanna rock, I-I wanna rock
right now*—so to them I come—struck dumb,
chime-blind, tolling with a throat full of Hosanna.
How many hours bowed against this Infinity of Blessed
Trinity? Communion of Pelvis, Sacrum, Femur.
My mouth—terrible angel, ever-lasting novena,
ecstatic devourer.

O, the places I have laid them, knelt and scooped
the amber—fast honey—from their openness,
Ah Muzen Cab's hidden Temple of Tulum—licked
smooth the sticky of her hip, heat-thrummed ossa
coxae. Lambent slave to ilium and ischium—I never tire
to shake this wild hive, split with thumb the sweet-
dripped comb—hot hexagonal hole, dark diamond—
to its nectar-dervished queen. Maenad tongue—
come-drunk hum-tranced honey-puller—for her hips,
I am—strummed-song and succubus.

They are the sign: hip. And the cosign: a great book—
the body's Bible opened up to its Good News Gospel.
*Alleluias, Ave Marías, madre mías, ay ay ays,
Ay Dios míos, and hip-hip-hooray.*

Cult of Coccyx. Culto de cadera.
Oracle of Orgasm. Rorschach's riddle:
What do I see? Hips:
Innominate bone. Wish bone. Orpheus bone.
Transubstantiation bone—hips of bread,
wine-whet thighs. *Say the word and healed I shall be*:
Bone butterfly. Bone wings. Bone Ferris wheel.

Bone basin bone throne bone lamp.
Apparition in the bone grotto—6th mystery,
slick rosary bead—*Deme la gracia* of a decade
in this garden of carmine flora. Exile me
to the enormous orchard of Alcinous—spiced fruit,
laden tree—Imparadise me. Because, God,
I am guilty. I am sin-frenzied and full of teeth
for pear upon apple upon fig.

More than all that are your hips.
They are a city. They are Kingdom.
Troy, the hollowed horse, an army of desire—
thirty soldiers in the belly, two in the mouth.
Beloved, your hips are the war.

At night your legs, love, are boulevards
leading me beggared and hungry to your candy
house, your baroque mansion. Even when I am late
and the tables have been cleared,
in the kitchen of your hips, let me eat cake.

O, constellation of pelvic glide—every curve,
a luster, a star. More infinite still, your hips
are kosmic, are universe—galactic carousel of burning
comets and big Big Bangs. Millennium Falcon,
let me be your Solo. O, hot planet, let me
circumambulate. O, spiral galaxy, I am coming
for your dark matter.

Along las calles de tus muslos I wander,
follow the parade of pulse like a drum line—
descend into your Plaza de Toros—
hands throbbing Miura bulls, dark Isleros.
Your arched hips—*ay, mi torera.*
Down the long corridor, your wet walls
lead me like a traje de luces—all glittered, glowed.
I am the animal born to rush your rich red
muletas—each breath, each sigh, each groan—

a hooked horn of want. My mouth at your inner
thigh. Here I must enter you, *mi pobre
Manolete*—press and part you like a wound—
make the crowd pounding in the grandstand
of your iliac crest rise up in you and cheer.

Top Ten Reasons Why Indians Are Good at Basketball

1.

The same reason we are good in bed.

2.

Because a long time ago, Creator gave us a choice: You can write like an Indian god, or you can have a jump shot sweeter than a 44oz. can of government grape juice—one or the other. Everyone but Sherman Alexie chose the jump shot.

3.

We know how to block shots, how to stuff them down your throat, because when you say, *Shoot*, we hear howitzer and Hotchkiss and Springfield Model 1873.

4.

When Indian ballers sweat, we emit a perfume of tortillas and Pine-Sol floor cleaner that works like a potion to disorient our opponents and make them forget their plays.

5.

We grew up knowing that there is no difference between a basketball court and church. Really, the Nazarenes hold church in the tribal gym on Sunday afternoons—the choir belts out "In the Sweet By and By" from the low block.

6.

When Walt Whitman wrote, *The half-breed straps on his light boots to compete in the race*, he really meant that all Indian men over age 40 have a pair of vintage Air Jordans in their closets and believe they are still magic-enough to make even the largest commod bod able to go coast to coast and finish a layup.

7.

Indians are not afraid to try sky hooks in real games, even though no Indian has ever made a sky hook, no Indian from a federally recognized tribe, anyway. But still, our shamelessness to attempt sky hooks in warm-ups strikes fear in our opponents, thus giving us a mental edge.

8.

On the court is the one place we will never be hungry—that net is an emptiness we can fill up all day long.

9.

We pretend we are playing every game for a Pendleton blanket, and the MVP gets a Mashantucket Pequot-sized per capita check.

10.

Really, though, all Indians are good at basketball because a basketball has never been just a basketball—it has always been a full moon in this terminal darkness, the one taillight in Jimmy Jack Tall Can's gray Granada cutting along the back dirt roads on a beer run, the Creator's heart that Coyote stole from the funeral pyre cursing him to walk alone through every coral dusk. It has always been a fat gourd we sing to, the left breast of a Mojave woman three Budweisers into Saturday night. It will always be a slick, bright bullet we can sling from the 3-point arc with 5 seconds left on a clock in the year 1492, and as it rips down through the net, our enemies will fall to their wounded knees, with torn ACLs.

That Which Cannot Be Stilled

Ash can make you clean,
        as alkaline as it is a grief.

My internet research calls it: *a disinfectant.*
        But life is faster research, and unavoidable.

Dirty Indian—a phrase blown like magnetite dust
        against the small bones in my ear, many times, and dark.

Sometimes I believed them—I'd look around
        my reservation, around our yard, our house—
                Dirty, I'd say,

like I was a doctor with a diagnosis,
        except I was the condition.

All my life I've been working,
        to get clean—to be clean is to be good, in America.
            To be clean is the grind.

Except my desert is made of sand, my skin
        the color of sand. It gets everywhere.

America is the condition—of the blood and of the rivers,

of what we can spill and who we can spill it from.
        A *dream* they call it, what is *American.*

Back home, we believe in dreams,
        heed what happens in fours as lucky.

Four iterations of any thing in a dream—
        a shade, an ancestor, a gesture, a cloud.

Four fat quails making a campanile of the mesquite tree.
        Four hands shuttling nighthawks along a loom
            of electrical wires.

I've had a recurring dream my entire life: It is night.
        I'm in the dunefield on the edge of the rez,
            tending each blue-gold mound smooth,

undisturbed. Each quartzed particle in its place—
        but a baby is crying in the green wooden crib,
            or someone is fighting someone else,

a quavering radio, a distempered dog.

I sorrow for silence: motion the dunes soft with my hands
        and *Please*, which is no invocation for peace.

I step lightly. I am holding my breath, maintaining,
        to keep it all from shifting.

Then it happens. Through what was perfect
        a carboned rubble sifts up—

tangled rebar, torn fences, scrambled,
        sheet metal, oxidized and spiking,
            breaking the sand like it's my own skin.

I feel the junk of it all in my body—a rising wild.
        I can't stop the happening. The rusting is in me,

like how a deep wound heals—glimmered, open.

There is no pattern of four in this dream,
        just *land and its moving*.

The dunes and how they are taken, reorganized
        and reckoned, grains loosened, Archimedes's myriad
            myriads, sifting in a coppered stream—

saltation, they call it, from Latin *saltare*, meaning *to jump* or *leap*.
        Isn't that what we do on the page?

John Ashbery died today, and tomorrow is my birthday.

Maybe death is a way to clean the self, of the body,
        to finally celebrate it. A celebration should leave a mess.

O, lit pyre of my anxiety,
        the ash-silver it streaks heavy across my chest and brow.
                The doctor asked, *Do you feel a sense of doom?*

Instead of replying, I wrote: What do you call a group of worms
        if not *a worry*, if not *a wonder*?

That was before I knew a dune has a *slip face* and a *slack*.

I have read more Ashbery today than I read when he lived—
        It's true that life can be anything, but certain things
                definitely aren't it,

like the red sugar horses and their satellite eyes,
        sphering and sick beneath the decks
                of your body, their ship.

We know how to speak to our conquerors, don't we?

What if you whisper into the long ear of one,
        say, *Beloved Occupier, Beloved Hoof*
                and Stiff Green Gallop.

Then tell them a story about the horse latitudes—
        a place so still not even the wind will go there.

That if they can't get it together, won't quit making a mess of you—
        those animals—won't stop carouseling
                your blood to hippodrome,

we might take them there, to some vast middle, lead them
    over the decks,

and far from the desert give them up to the sea,
    watch the slow green-blue dunes lift open
        and disrupt everything, which cannot be stilled.

The First Water Is the Body

The Colorado River is the most endangered river in the United States—also, it is a part of my body.

I carry a river. It is who I am: 'Aha Makav. This is not metaphor.

When a Mojave says, *Inyech 'Aha Makavch ithuum*, we are saying our name. We are telling a story of our existence. *The river runs through the middle of my body.*

So far, I have said the word *river* in every stanza. I don't want to waste water. I must preserve the river in my body.

In future stanzas, I will try to be more conservative.

↠

The Spanish called us, *Mojave. Colorado*, the name they gave our river because it was silt-red-thick.

Natives have been called *red* forever. I have never met a red Native, not even on my reservation, not even at the National Museum of the American Indian, not even at the largest powwow in Parker, Arizona.

I live in the desert along a dammed blue river. The only red people I've seen are white tourists sunburned after staying out on the water too long.

↞

'Aha Makav is the true name of our people, given to us by our Creator who loosed the river from the earth and built it into our living bodies.

Translated into English, *'Aha Makav* means *the river runs through the middle of our body, the same way it runs through the middle of our land.*

This is a poor translation, like all translations.

In American imaginations, the logic of this image will lend itself to surrealism or magical realism—

Americans prefer a magical red Indian, or a shaman, or a fake Indian in a red dress, over a real Native. Even a real Native carrying the dangerous and heavy blues of a river in her body.

What threatens white people is often dismissed as myth. I have never been true in America. America is my myth.

↠

Jacques Derrida says, *Every text remains in mourning until it is translated.*

When Mojaves say the word for *tears*, we return to our word for *river*, as if our river were flowing from our eyes. *A great weeping* is how you might translate it. Or *a river of grief.*

But who is this translation for and will they come to my language's four-night funeral to grieve what has been lost in my efforts at translation? When they have drunk dry my river will they join the mourning procession across our bleached desert?

The word for *drought* is different across many languages and lands. The ache of thirst, though, translates to all bodies along the same paths—the tongue, the throat, the kidneys. No matter what language you speak, no matter the color of your skin.

↞

We carry the river, its body of water, in our body.

I do not mean to imply a visual relationship. Such as: a Native woman on her knees holding a box of Land O' Lakes butter whose label has a picture of a Native woman on her knees holding a box of Land O' Lakes butter whose label has a picture of a Native woman on her knees . . .

We carry the river, its body of water, in our body. I do not mean to invoke the Droste effect—this is not a picture of a river within a picture of a river.

I mean *river* as a verb. A happening. It is moving within me right now.

→

This is not juxtaposition. Body and water are not *two unlike things*—they are more than *close together or side by side*. They are *same*—body, being, energy, prayer, current, motion, medicine.

The body is beyond six senses. Is sensual. An ecstatic state of energy, always on the verge of praying, or entering any river of movement.

Energy is a moving river moving my moving body.

←

In Mojave thinking, body and land are the same. The words are separated only by the letters 'ii and 'a: 'iimat for body, 'amat for land. In conversation, we often use a shortened form for each: *mat-*. Unless you know the context of a conversation, you might not know if we are speaking about our body or our land. You might not know which has been injured, which is remembering, which is alive, which was dreamed, which needs care. You might not know we mean both.

If I say, *My river is disappearing*, do I also mean, *My people are disappearing?*

→

How can I translate—not in words but in belief—that a river is a body, as alive as you or I, that there can be no life without it?

←

John Berger wrote, *True translation is not a binary affair between two languages but a triangular affair. The third point of the triangle being what lay behind the words of the original text before it was written. True translation demands a return to the pre-verbal.*

Between the English translation I offered, and the urgency I felt typing ʻAha Makav in the lines above, is not the point where this story ends or begins.

We must go to the place before those two points—we must go to the third place that is the river.

We must go to the point of the lance entering the earth, and the river becoming the first body bursting from earth's clay body into my sudden body. We must submerge, come under, beneath those once warm red waters now channeled blue and cool, the current's endless yards of emerald silk wrapping the body and moving it, swift enough to take life or give it.

We must go until we smell the black root-wet anchoring the river's mud banks. We must go beyond beyond to a place where we have never been the center, where there is no center—beyond, toward what does not need us yet makes us.

↠

What is this third point, this place that breaks a surface, if not the deep-cut and crooked bone bed where the Colorado River runs—a one-thousand-four-hundred-and-fifty-mile thirst—into and through a body?

Berger called it the *pre-verbal. Pre-verbal* as in the body when the body was more than body. Before it could name itself *body* and be limited, bordered by the space *body* indicated.

Pre-verbal is the place where the body was yet a green-blue energy greening, greened and bluing the stone, red and floodwater, the razorback fish, the beetle, and the cottonwoods' and willows' shaded shadows.

Pre-verbal was when the body was more than a body and possible.

One of its possibilities was to hold a river within it.

←

A river is a body of water. It has a foot, an elbow, a mouth. It runs. It lies in a bed. It can make you good. It has a head. It remembers everything.

→

If I was created to hold the Colorado River, to carry its rushing inside me, if the very shape of my throat, of my thighs is for wetness, how can I say who I am if the river is gone?

What does 'Aha Makav mean if the river is emptied to the skeleton of its fish and the miniature sand dunes of its dry silten beds?

If the river is a ghost, am I?

Unsoothable thirst is one type of haunting.

←

A phrase popular or more known to non-Natives during the Standing Rock encampment was, *Water is the first medicine*. It is true.

Where I come from we cleanse ourselves in the river. I mean: *The water makes us strong* and able to move forward into what is set before us to do with good energy.

We cannot live good, we cannot live at all, without water.

If we poison and use up our water, how will we clean our wounds and our wrongs? How will we wash away what we must leave behind us? How will we make ourselves new?

→

To thirst and to drink is how one knows they are alive and grateful.

To thirst and then not drink is . . .

←

If your builder could place a small red bird in your chest to beat as your heart, is it so hard for you to picture the blue river hurtling inside the slow muscled curves of my long body? Is it too difficult to believe it is as sacred as a breath or a star or a sidewinder or your own mother or your beloveds?

If I could convince you, would our brown bodies and our blue rivers be more loved and less ruined?

The Whanganui River in New Zealand now has the same legal rights of a human being. In India, the Ganges and Yamuna Rivers now have the same legal status of a human being. Slovenia's constitution now declares access to clean drinking water to be a national human right. While in the United States, we are teargassing and rubber-bulleting and kenneling Natives trying to protect their water from pollution and contamination at Standing Rock in North Dakota. We have yet to discover what the effects of lead-contaminated water will be on the children of Flint, Michigan, who have been drinking it for years.

→

America is a land of bad math and science. The Right believes Rapture will save them from the violence they are delivering upon the earth and water; the Left believes technology, the same technology wrecking the earth and water, will save them from the wreckage or help them build a new world on Mars.

←

We think of our bodies as being all that we are: *I am my body.* This thinking helps us disrespect water, air, land, one another. But water is not external from our body, our self.

My Elder says, *Cut off your ear, and you will live. Cut off your hand, you will live. Cut off your leg, you can still live. Cut off our water, we will not live more than a week.*

The water we drink, like the air we breathe, is not a part of our body but is our body. What we do to one—to the body, to the water—we do to the other.

↠

Toni Morrison writes, *All water has a perfect memory and is forever trying to get back to where it was.* Back to the body of earth, of flesh, back to the mouth, the throat, back to the womb, back to the heart, to its blood, back to our grief, back back back.

Will we remember from where we've come? The water.

And once remembered, will we return to that first water, and in doing so return to ourselves, to each other?

Do you think the water will forget what we have done, what we continue to do?

Didn't they tell you that I was a savage?

ROBYN FENTY

I, Minotaur

I am an invention—dark alarm,
Briareus's hands striking the bells of my blood.
      Whose toll am I?

      I think too much—
each morning the Minotauromachy.
Through the night I swing the sickle of my wonders,
      a harvest-work—of touch and worry.
Spend dawn and its day burning my dead—
      Who fell in the night? What the night reaped?

I am every answer—
a mathematics of anxiety. How any maul can solve
      the mesquite tree for the pyre.

      In my chest I am two-hearted always—
love and what love becomes
      arrive when they want to, and hungry.
The locusts disappeared the fields then themselves.
I bent—wept alone on the threshing floor,
      not for what went stick to the feast—
I wept for the locusts.

I know what it's like to be appetite of your own appetite,
      citizen of what savages you,
to dare bloom pleasure from your wounds—
      and to bleed out from that bouquet.

A head like mine was shaped on thirst.
      I dream what is wet or might quench—
        aquifers, rivers, cenotes, canals.
The dusked mirage of lake above your knee I sip and lick—
      my tongue blush as the fluoresced ear of a jackrabbit.

I obey what I don't understand, then I become it,
    which needs no understanding.
The astonishment of my body's limits—
how it is easily divided by a black field,
        and the black field multiplied in stars.
The throng of a lover constellating.

Like any desert, I learn myself by what's desired of me—
        and I am demoned by those desires.
For this, I move like a wound—always, and fruiting,
    sweetened by the thorn.

The tumbleweed turns and turns,
until it bursts free all its spores into the wind,
        until it is only what it might become.
There is no such thing as time or June,
    only what you're born into—
only waiting for the rain, for the flood,
for what erupts my badlands and my tired eyes in beauty—
        Mojave aster, desert globemallow,
where once was terrible nothing.

There is no god here in these flesh-hours,
    though your jaw is a temple and your hips
        strike like an axe—
the labrys I injure myself against.

        But you called to here by me come softly,
into the bull-noon of my body—
    and not unknowingly.
You've heard me churn and lather, yet knock and enter.
Together we are the color of magnets,
    and also their doing. Manganese, lodestone,
ores the light will not touch, so we touch the light—
        give it to one another
until we are riddled and leaking with it.

What else can we prostrate
　　　　or set before the large feet of our creators
if not the diminishment of the body—this *Book of Scars*.

Sand grinds like gears between my teeth—
　　　　sparkling, small machinery of want.
What question can I ask of the thing I am?
　　　　All I have done and failed to do.
The furrows I tear with my grief-mouth, a map of myself
　　　　carved by my own horns.

I have a name, yet no one who will say it not roughly.
　　　　I am your Native,
and this is my American labyrinth.
Here I am, at your thighs—lilac-lit pools of ablution.
　　　　Take my body and make of it—
　　　　　　a Nation, a confession.
Through you even I can be clean.

It Was the Animals

Today my brother brought over a piece of the ark
wrapped in a white plastic grocery bag.

He set the bag on my dining table, unknotted it,
peeled it away, revealing a foot-long fracture of wood.
He took a step back and gestured toward it
with his arms and open palms—

> *It's the ark*, he said.
> *You mean Noah's ark?* I asked.
> *What other ark is there?* he answered.

> *Read the inscription*, he told me.
> *It tells what's going to happen at the end.*
> *What end?* I wanted to know.
> He laughed, *What do you mean, 'What end?'*
> *The end end.*

Then he lifted it out. The plastic bag rattled.
His fingers were silkened by pipe blisters.
He held the jagged piece of wood so gently.
I had forgotten my brother could be gentle.

He set it on the table the way people on television
set things when they're afraid those things might blow up
or go off—he set it right next to my empty coffee cup.

It was no ark—
it was the broken end of a picture frame
with a floral design carved into its surface.

He put his head in his hands—

I shouldn't show you this—
God, why did I show her this?
It's ancient—O, God,
this is so old.

Fine, I gave in. *Where did you get it?*
The girl, he said. *O, the girl.*
What girl? I asked.
You'll wish you never knew, he told me.

I watched him drag his wrecked fingers
over the chipped flower-work of the wood—

You should read it. But, O, you can't take it—
no matter how many books you've read.

He was wrong. I could take the ark.
I could even take his marvelously fucked fingers.
The way they almost glittered.

It was the animals—the animals I could not take—

they came up the walkway into my house,
cracked the doorframe with their hooves and hips,
marched past me, into my kitchen, into my brother,

tails snaking across my feet before disappearing
like retracting vacuum cords into the hollows
of my brother's clavicles, tusks scraping the walls,

reaching out for him—wildebeests, pigs,
the oryxes with their black matching horns,
javelinas, jaguars, pumas, raptors. The ocelots
with their mathematical faces. So many kinds of goat.
So many kinds of creature.

I wanted to follow them, to get to the bottom of it,
but my brother stopped me—

    This is serious, he said.
    You have to understand.
    It can save you.

So I sat down, with my brother ruined open like that,
and two by two the fantastical beasts
parading him. I sat, as the water fell against my ankles,
built itself up around me, filled my coffee cup
before floating it away from the table.

My brother—teeming with shadows—
a hull of bones, lit by tooth and tusk,
lifting his ark high in the air.

How the Milky Way Was Made

My river was once unseparated. Was Colorado. Red-
fast flood. Able to take

   anything it could wet—in a wild rush—

     all the way to Mexico.

Now it is shattered by fifteen dams
over one thousand four hundred and fifty miles,

pipes and pumps filling
swimming pools and sprinklers

   in Los Angeles and Las Vegas.

To save our fish, we lifted them from our skeletoned river beds,
loosed them in our heavens, set them aster—

   'Achii 'ahan, Mojave salmon,

     Colorado pike minnow.

Up there they glide gilled with stars.
You see them now—

   god-large, gold-green sides,

     lunar-white belly to breast—

making their great speeded way across the darkest hours,
rippling the sapphired sky-water into a galaxy road.

The blurred wake they drag as they make their path
through the night sky is called

'Achii 'ahan nyuunye—

our words for *Milky Way.*

Coyote too is up there, locked in the moon
after his failed attempt to leap it, fishing net wet

and empty slung over his back—

a prisoner blue and dreaming

of unzipping the salmon's silked skins with his teeth.
O, the weakness of any mouth

as it gives itself away to the universe

of a sweet-milk body.

As my own mouth is dreamed to thirst
the long desire-ways, the hundred thousand light-year roads

of your wrists and thighs.

exhibits from The American Water Museum

0.
I can't tell you anything new about the river—
you can't tell a river to itself.

17.
A recording plays from somewhere high,
or low, floating up or down through the falling
dust-light.

It is a voice out of time, voice of quickness,
voice of glass—or wind. A melody, almost—of mud.
How it takes a deep blue to tumble wet stones
into a songline. The music any earth makes
when touched and shaped by the original green energy.
The song, if translated, might feel like this:

> You have been made in my likeness.
>
> I am inside you—I am you / or you are me.
>
> Let us say to one another: *I am yours*—
>
> and know finally that we will only ever be
>
> as much as we are willing to save of one another.

4.
The guidebook's single entry:

> *There is no guide.*
> *You built this museum.*
> *You have always been*
> *its Muse and Master.*

5.
Admission is general and free
except for what the children pay—
and they pay in the kidneys.

99.
From an original rock painting in Topock, Arizona, now digitized on a
wall-mounted monitor:

Before this city, the Creator pressed his staff
into the earth, and the earth opened—

it wasn't a wound, it was joy—joy!—!
Out of this opening leaped earth's most radical bloom: *our people*—

we blossoms from the original body: water,
flowering and flowing until it became itself, and we, us:
                              River. Body.

78.
The first violence against any body of water
is to forget the name its creator first called it.
Worse: forget the bodies who spoke that name.

An American way of forgetting Natives:
Discover them with City. Crumble them by City.
Erase them into Cities named for their bones, until

you are the new Natives of your new Cities.
Let the new faucets run in celebration, in excess.
Who lies beneath streets, universities, art museums?

                    My people!

I learn to love them from up here, through concrete.
La llorona out on the avenues crying for everyone's
babies, for all the mothers, including River, grinded

to their knees and dust for the splendid City. Still,
we must sweep the dust, gather our own bodies like
messes of sand and memory. Who will excavate

our clodded bodies from the banks, pick embedded
stones and sticks from the raw scrapes oozing
our backs and thighs? Who will call us back

to the water, wash the dirt from our eyes and hair?
Can anybody uncrush our hands, reshape them
from clay, let us touch one another's faces again?

Has anyone answered? We've been crying out
for 600 years—

> *Tengo sed.*

204.
A dilapidated diorama of the mythical city of Flint, Michigan:

The glue that once held the small-scale balsa wood children
to their places—along the streets, waiting in line at the bus stop,
on top of the slide in a playground, or on the basketball court—
has desiccated and snapped away. Now the children lie flat on
the floor of the diorama, like they are sleeping, open-eyed
to the sight, to what they have seen through their mouths—
hundreds of miniature empty clay cups roll back and forth
out of reach of their hands, some have ground down to tinier
piles of dust and sand at their unmoving fingertips.

23.
River, an interactive performance piece:

> *Sit or stand silently. Close your eyes until they are still.*
> *In the stillness breathe in the river moving inside you.*
> *It is a thick smell, a color. Touch it—not with your hands,*
> *but with your entire sensual skin. Touch it with your flesh.*

*Drink from yourself until you are full. Realize the emptiness
made by your fullness. . . . No, no, no—Don't repent. This is
a museum not a church.*

123.
Marginalia from the BIA Watermongers Congressional Records, redacted:

To kill ▮▮▮▮ take their water
To kill ▮▮▮▮ steal their water
            then tell them how much they owe
To kill ▮▮▮▮ bleed them of what is wet in them
To kill ▮▮▮▮ find their river and slit its throat
To kill ▮▮▮▮ pollute their water with their daughters'
            busted drowned bodies washed up
            on the shores, piece by piece

205.
The water piped into every American city is called *dead water.*

300.
There is a urinal inside a curtained booth in the corner.
The lit sign above the curtain hums and flickers: *Donations.*

You have nothing to give.

10.
Metonymic Experience:

There are more than 60,000 miles of waterways in our bodies—
veins, arteries—the red lines of our own lives. We are
topographies of sustainable greed—*dragons be here now,*
in our bellies, in the cracked bowl bottoms of lakebeds,
bloodshot eyes frayed like red speaker wires scorched
in the sun. We thirst. Our thirst is a caravan—pilgrims of

scarcity. As we die of drought, we splay in the shifting sand
like old maps to follow, ones that led us here to begin with,
brought us to this masterpiece of thirst, as architects and
social practice artists. The curators ask us to collapse
as naturally as possible, in a heap—so those who come
behind us might be immersed in this exhibit of thirst,
as if it was their own.

Soon.

67.
There are grief counselors on site for those who realize
they have entered The American Water Museum not as
patrons but rather as parts of the new exhibit.

68.
The drinking fountain blows a metallic blue ribbon from its spout.

41.
Embroidered martyr banners hang in the entryway:
A swath of cloth and flag for the rivers who refused
American citizenry, who would not speak English,
no matter how badly they were beaten and bled.

7.
Text RVR followed by # to sign up for the text message survey:

What does a day feel like when you're nourished
on the bodies and fleshes of those felled for your
arrival? A butterfly sipping on the opened neck
of a horse stiffening beneath the mottled shade
wept by a cottonwood tree? What does it mean
that your life is made of someone else's shed
water and blood? Dial 1 if you don't care.

874.
Blueprints from another water restoration project:

Faint lines of freeway overpass and surrounding houses.
The kidney-shape of a pond circled by a concrete path.
Sketches of a ramada, a parking lot, fake visitors, toy cars . . .

Graffitied in red spray paint across the blueprints:

> *This once-river has not been restored to itself—*
> *it is a river and still isn't a river.*

2345.*
The river is my sister—I am its daughter.
It is my hands when I drink from it,
my own eye when I am weeping,
and my desire when I ache like a yucca bell
in the night. The river says, *Open your mouth to me,*
and I will make you more.

Because even a river can be lonely,
> *even a river will die of thirst.*

I am both—the river and its vessel.
It maps me alluvium. A net of moon-colored fish.
I've flashed through it like copper wire.

A cottonwood root swelling with drink,
I tremble every leaf to lime, every bean to gold,
jingle the willow in the same song the river sings.

I am it and its mud.
I am the body kneeling at the river's edge
letting it drink from me.

---

* The prayer of an Elder Mojave woman shot in the head and throat by two rubber bullets as she sat in prayer before a tractor and a row of German shepherds barking against their leashes at the site of yet another pipeline.

200.
You cannot drink poetry.

19.
There is often trouble choosing which language for the headset:

Makav: 'Aha Haviily inyep nyuwiich.
Español: A beber y a tragar, que el mundo se va a acabar.

I am fluent in water. Water is fluent in my body—
it spoke my body into existence.

If a river spoke English, it might say:

> *What begins in water*
> *will end without it.*

Or,

> *I remember you—*
> *I cannot forget*
>   *my own body.*

88.*
You remember everything,
carve a waterline of my transgressions,
and despite all I've done,
you've suffered to return to me.
You've fed the mesquite's thorns
and the sweet of its glowing beans.

You've pulled me under and released me clean.
You made me new, something better than good.

---

* The last love letter written to the last river. It was the wish of the last river that the letter not be made public until 100 years after her death.

Like me you are a fast body.
A coppery current.
I laid in your bed.
I kept you for myself
except you are myself
and kept me instead.

365.
Photograph from a South American newspaper:

US-headquartered companies bought the rights
to water in other countries. These companies are
strangers to the gods of those waters, were not
formed from them, have never said *Gracias* to
those waters, never prayed to those waters
have never been cleansed by those waters.

The US-headquartered companies announce,
with armed guards, *You can't drink from this lake
anymore.* The Natives gather rain instead, open
their beautiful water-shaped mouths to the sky,
catch it in curved, peach-colored shells, in halved
gourds, in their water-shaped hands.

The companies say, *Read these documents—
we bought the rain too.*

> *We own the rain.*

210.
The Credible Thirst Interview:

When did you first enter the territory of thirst?

How many days have you waited in the long line
of thirst with your dirty jug?

Are you able to love anyone—
your mother, your son, your lover—
in the midst of such hunger and this fire
stretching out and lengthening your throat?

How many bodies have you pressed into,
not for desire but for the saliva you sucked
from their tongue?

Have you leaned your head against the miles
and miles of cyclone fence to steady the dizziness,
to slow the breath and thud at your temples,
the mirages, and hallucinations?

Have you ever considered your thirst as a weapon?

Do you now consider yourself a soldier
in the battle for something wet?

Do you recall in how many instances
you didn't care when it was
someone else's thirst erupting?

And now: Who should fill your cup
from their own jug?

211.
There are differing opinions about how kissing
became criminal. Who hasn't drunk,
hasn't begged at the well of a lover's mouth?
Love has never been different from thirst,
but now everything is different. All the cups
are filled with dirt—even our mouths.

3000.
Water remembers everything it travels over and through.
If you have been in water, part of you remains there still.

It is a memoir of an indissoluble relationship with the world.
But where is water now? Where is the world?

301.
The Magic Show:

Only water can change water, can heal itself. Not even God
made water. Not on any of the seven days. It was already here.
Or maybe God is water, because I am water, and you are water.

11.
Art of Fact:

Let me tell you a story about water:
Once upon a time there was us.
America's thirst tried to drink us away.
And here we still are.

Isn't the Air Also a Body, Moving?

It holds the red jet of the hawk
     in its hand of dust.
How is it that we know what we are?
If not by the air
    between any hand and its want—touch.

I am touched—I am.
     This is my knee, since she touches me there.
     This is my throat, as defined by her reaching.

What pressure—the air.
     Buoying me now along a minute
the size of a strange room.
Who knew air could be so treacherous
    to move through? An old, anxious sea,

or waking too early in a coppered
     and indigo morning,
or the bookmark she left
near the end of the book—
all deep blues and euphemisms
    for my anxieties.

Sometimes I don't know how to make it
to the other side of the bridge of atoms
    of a second. Except for the air

breathing me, inside, then out. Suddenly,
    I am still here.
Escaping must be like this
for the magician and mortal both—
    like lungs and air. A trick

of bones and leaving any capture—a breath.
    Everything is iron oxide or red this morning,

here in Sedona. The rocks, my love's mouth,
     even the chapel and its candles. Red.
I have been angry this week. Christian said,
Trust your anger. It is a demand for love.
    Or it is red. Red is a thing

I can trust—a monster and her wings,
     cattle grazing the sandstone hills like flames.

Caboose cars were once red,
     and also the best parts of the trains—
the heat and shake of what promised to pass.
    Finally, the red and the end of them.

Maybe this living is a balance of drunkenness
off nitrogen and the unbearable
     atmosphere of memory.

From the right distance, I can hold anything
     in my hand—the hawk riding a thermal,
the horizon which across many days might lead to
    the sea, the red cliff, my love

glazed in fine red dust, your letter, even the train.
    Each is devoured in its own envelope of air.
What we hold grows weight,
    becomes enough or burden.

Cranes, Mafiosos, and a Polaroid Camera

I had a few days left of my stay at the crane sanctuary
in Kearney, Nebraska, when my brother called. It was 3:24 a.m.
It's me, he said. *It's your brother.* He had taken apart

another Polaroid camera and needed me to explain how
to put it back together. His voice was a snare drum, knocking
and quick. He was crying. I didn't want to wake the other visitors,

and I knew he'd keep calling, hour after hour, day after day,
lifetime after miserable lifetime, until I answered. I slid out of bed.
Tell me what to do. You know what to do, he pleaded.

I should know how to help my brother by now. He and I
have had this exact conversation before—if I love him,
if I really love him, why haven't I learned to reassemble

a Polaroid camera? Instead, I told him about the sandhill cranes,
the way they dance—moving into and giving way to one another,
bowing down, cresting and collapsing their wings,

necks and shoulders silver curls of smoky rhythm—
but he didn't believe me. My brother believes the mafia
placed a transmitter deep within his Polaroid camera,

but he can't believe in dancing cranes. *You think this is a joke?*
he whispers. *These are fucking Mafiosos I'm talking about.
You're probably next.* He hung up on me.

That dawn, I aimed my digital camera at the sky
until the last of an island of late-rising cranes lifted into the metallic
air—I couldn't take my eyes from the barrel of lens, my finger,

fast trigger against the black skeleton of the camera. I wondered
what it would look like cracked open to its upside-down mirrors
and polished levers, how many screws there were, how many lantern-lit

cranes might come unfurling out of that cage. I wondered
what I would look like if the darkened chambers of my body
were unlocked. What streams of light might escape me and reveal

about the things I collect and hide, and is there a difference
between aperture and wound. Mostly, I wondered where
my brother keeps getting those goddamned Polaroid cameras.

The Cure for Melancholy Is to Take the Horn

Powdered unicorn horn was once thought to cure melancholy.

What carries the hurt is never the wound
    but the red garden sewn by the horn
as it left—and she left. I am rosing,
    blossoming absence—a brilliant alarum.

Brodsky said, *Darkness restores what light cannot
    repair.* You thrilled me—torn to the comb.
I want everything—the ebon bull and the moon.
    I come and again for the honeyed horn.

Queen Elizabeth traded a castle for a single horn.
    I serve the kingdom of my hands—
an army of touch marching the alcázar of your thighs
    blaring and bright as any war horn.

I arrive at you—half bestia, half feast.
    Night after night we harvest the luxed Bosque
de Caderas, reap the darkful fruit mulling our mouths,
    separate sweet from thorn.

My lanternist. Your hands wick at the bronzed
    lamp of my breast. Strike me to spark—
tremble me to awe. Into your lap
    let me lay my heavy horns.

I fulfilled the prophecy of your throat, loosed in you
    the fabulous wing of my mouth. Red holy-red
ghost. Left my body and spoke to God, came back
    seraphimed—copper feathered and horned.

Our bodies are nothing if not places to be had by,
    as in, *God, she had me by the throat,*
by the hip bone, by the moon. God,
    she hurt me with my own horns.

Waist and Sway

I never meant to break—

but streetlights dressed her gold.
The curve and curve of her shoulders—
the hum and hive of them,
moonglossed pillory of them—
nearly felled me to my knees.

How can I tell you—the amber of her.
The body of honey—I took it in my hands.

Oh, City—where hands turned holy—

her city, where my hands went undone—
gone to ravel, to silhouette, to moths at the mercy
of the pale of her hips. Hips that in the early night
to light lit up—to shining sweet electricus,
to luminous and lamp—where ached to drink
I did till drunk.

Where in her rocked the dark Zikmund—
her, by then, a cathedral tower.
One breast, rose window.
One breast, room of alchemists.
Where from her came a tolling—
the music of yoke and crown,
of waist and sway.

Wanting her was so close to prayer—
I should not. But it was July,
and in a city where desire means, *Upstairs
we can break each other open,*
the single blessing I had to give was *Mouth*—
so gave and gave I did.

Every night has a woman for temptation.
Every city has a fable for fruit—
like in the castle gardens, where jackdaws waited
glaze-eyed along the walls for a taste of new—
of figs unsweet yet, yet beryl-bright
enough for wonder.

Not jackdaw, but not different, I—how I destroy myself
on even the least of the sweetest things—
the salt of her burned not long on my tongue,
but like stars.

I never meant to break—but love,
the hymn and bells of her.

Even now, there are nights I climb the narrow stairway
to an apartment at Hradčany Square, where a door opens
to a room and the shadowed fig of her mouth—
cleaved sweet open, and in me ringing.

If I Should Come Upon Your House Lonely in the West Texas Desert

I will swing my lasso of headlights
across your front porch,

let it drop like a rope of knotted light
at your feet.

While I put the car in park,
you will tie and tighten the loop

of light around your waist—
and I will be there with the other end

wrapped three times
around my hips horned with loneliness.

Reel me in across the glow-throbbing sea
of greenthread, bluestem prickly poppy,

the white inflorescence of yucca bells,
up the dust-lit stairs into your arms.

If you say to me, *This is not your new house
but I am your new home,*

I will enter the door of your throat,
hang my last lariat in the hallway,

build my altar of best books on your bedside table,
turn the lamp on and off, on and off, on and off.

I will lie down in you.
Eat my meals at the red table of your heart.

Each steaming bowl will be, *Just right.*
I will eat it all up,

break all your chairs to pieces.
If I try running off into the deep-purpling scrub brush,

you will remind me,
There is nowhere to go if you are already here,

and pat your hand on your lap lighted
by the topazion lux of the moon through the window,

say, *Here, Love, sit here*—when I do,
I will say, *And here I still am.*

Until then, Where are you? What is your address?
I am hurting. I am riding the night

on a full tank of gas and my headlights
are reaching out for something.

Snake-Light

I can read a text in anything.

To read a body is to break that body a little.

When my desert reads a life out loud
it takes the body down, back to caliche and clay,
one symbol at a time—

the blue milk of an eye sipped empty,
a wasted tongue rewinding to its vacant throat,
each vertebra unlocked and dragged beneath the sand.

The body after itself, the after-body—

undressed to its banquet,
for yellow jackets and butterflies. Yes, butterflies
nourish on the nectar

and the wrack—ascending, descending,
against the snake's broken body, in adoration.

The devotional fervor-work of revision.

Let's say it's all text—the animal, the dune,
the wind in the cottonwood, and the body.

Everything *book*: a form bound together.
This is also *book*: the skeleton of a rattlesnake

sheathed tightly in its unopened flesh.
Apex of spine and spur, the wet-black
curves of unlit bone, dark parentheses—letters

flexed across a mica-lit gulley, a line.
What is a page if not a lingering, an opaque
waiting—to be marked, and written?

Even the rattlesnake is legible
through the muscled strike of its body.
A sentence, or a spell, a taut rope of emotion—

serpentine signal against the surface of the eye's
moon-stroked desert floor.

↞

In the woods with my love, there was a snakeskin
dangling from the tree bark. Sleeve of gold, honey-
combed, scaled with light.

I touched it softly—the way I touch a line while reading—
trembling with the body of the snake before it left itself,
like leaving one word for the next—becoming, and possible.

I gave the skin to my love and said, *Now I am a story—
like the snake, I am my own future.*

↠

Lines are shed like snakeskin—rubbed against
the rough white page, released. Not remembered
or unremembered. The body leaving itself for itself.

Each new line its own body, made possible
by the first body, and here now entering
the rooms of our eye and ear.

The new body is how the rattlesnake knows itself—
not as less body but as whole body.

↞

You should never kill a rattlesnake—
a rattlesnake is also human.

↠

Americans worship their obsessions in violent ways—
they write them down.

Americans celebrate the rattlesnake in rattlesnake rodeos—
round them up, kill them, sell them. Cash prizes
for the heaviest and longest rattlesnake, more cash
for the most dead rattlesnakes.

Rattlesnakes skinned to their tails, torsos rewritten
as italic slope, meat darkening and arched
among the almost-white prairie grasses—
the rattlesnake read and interpreted, rendered

a classic American character in a classic American font.

↞

In my Mojave language, when you desire
the rattlesnake, you call out its first name,

>   *Hikwiir.*
You can't know the rattlesnake's power

if you've never felt its first name stretch and strike
in your mouth—like making lightning,

unfolding fangs from the soft palate of your jaw,
delivering all of it to a body you want to pull inside you:

her mouth, her throat, in your mouth and throat,
her shoulders and ribcage—

you would fold her in half if you could—
hips, such a long thigh, thigh, calves, ankles.

And afterward, you are changed,
bewildered, slow.

↠

In the beginning, the letter N
was the image of a snake.

Phoenician scribes held it in their hands, gave it.
They deepened the body's curve
and chopped off the snake's head,
which didn't change the body's song.

↞

When I write my name
I hold the cool, scaled body
of the snake. Set it writhing
on the page—*N*, it sings.

Beneath the patterns burnishing
the rattlesnake's back, its pale belly
glows—page, a place of hunger.
Some days the N is silent
without its head. It's the *Hnnnh*
of the scribe's sword I hear
written in my ear.

↠

I have another name—
I have a rattlesnake name.

When you say my name, you mean, *The rattlesnake
is sitting there, watching, waiting, for her.*

I am also *her.*

My Elder says, *You are like that rattlesnake.*
She is quiet, quiet. Then she strikes, and it's too late.

You can rewrite but not unwrite.

↢

The rattlesnake. I. Are ampersand.
A coil, almost.

We, ligature.

↠

When a snake swallows its prey,
a row of inner teeth help walk the jaw
over the prey's body—walking like reading.

Walking over a word with the teeth of our mind.

To write is to be eaten. To read, to be full.

↢

The rattlesnake moves like sepia ink.
The white muscle of the page is what makes these dark ribs walk.
The dimmed bone line is still.
Somewhere deep—the rattle of energy, the hibernaculum.

↠

I watched a rattlesnake swim across the Colorado River,
down near the Devil's Elbow, where the sea monster,
whose name I cannot tell you, turned the mountain to sand—
created a 90-degree bend in the course of the blue-green water.

◄◄

I dream of snakes who want to speak to me.
I cover my ears, I run.

I jumped in the bed of a red pickup truck.
The snake stood up on its tail, human.
It spoke with its black tongue like a flick
of black hair in the wind.

It spoke to me with that tongue,
making all those black knots in the air.

►►

The alphabet of my love's hand in the dark,
a gesture I can read. A desire-text.
She enters me—I am her scriptorium.

◄◄

My Tío Facundo was from Zacatecas,
and skinned a rattlesnake in our backyard.
Fried it in el disco. He gave me the rattle
tied on a cord I wore around my neck.
Until my Mojave great grandmother saw it,
said, *Take it off.* I asked, *Why?* She said,
Would you wear my foot around your neck?
I said, *You don't have feet.* She said, *Take it off.*
She said, *We don't eat snakes. They are our sisters.*

She said, *I gave you my name—I called you.*
And I watched her tongue like a whip of ink
write my name in the air.

My Brother, My Wound

He was calling in the bulls from the street.
They came like a dark river,
a flood of chest and hoof.
Everything moving, under, splinter. Hooked
their horns though the walls. Light hummed
the holes like yellow jackets. My mouth
was a nest torn empty.

Then, he was at the table.
Then, in the pig's jaws.
He was not hungry. He was stop.
He was bad apple. He was choking.

So I punched my fists against his stomach.
Mars flew out
and broke open or bloomed.
How many small red eyes shut in that husk?

He said, *Look. Look.* And they did.

He said, *Lift up your shirt.* And I did.

He slid his fork between my ribs.
Yes, he sang. *A Jesus side wound.*
It wouldn't stop bleeding.
He reached inside
and turned on the lamp.

I never knew I was also a lamp, until the light
fell out of me, dripped down my thigh,
flew up in me, caught in my throat like a canary.
Canaries really means dogs, he said.

He put on his shoes.
You started this with your mouth, he pointed.
Where are you going? I asked.
To ride the Ferris wheel, he answered,
and climbed inside me like a window.

¿Qué me admiro?

¿Quién en amor ha sido más dichoso?

SOR JUANA INÉS DE LA CRUZ

Grief Work

Why not now go toward the things I love?

I have walked slow in the garden
of her—: gazed the black flower

        dilating her animal-
        eye.

I give up my sorrows
the way a bull gives its horns—: astonished,

        and wishing there is rest
        in the body's softest parts.

Like Jacob's angel, I touched the garnet
of her hip,

        and she knew my name,
        and I knew hers—:

it was *Auxocromo*, it was *Cromóforo*,
it was *Eliza*.

When the eyes and lips are brushed with honey
what is seen and said will never be the same,

so why not take the apple
in your mouth—:

        in flames, in pieces, straight
        from the knife's sharp edge?

Achilles chased Hektor around the walls
of Ilium three times—: how long must I circle

the high gate
between her hip and knee

       to solve the red-gold geometry
       of her thigh?

Again the gods put their large hands in me,
move me, break my heart

like a clay jug of wine, loosen a beast
from some darklong depth.

       My melancholy is hoofed.
       I, the terrible beautiful

Lampon, a shining devour-horse tethered
at the bronze manger of her collarbones.

       I do my grief work
       with her body—:

labor to make the emerald tigers
in her throat leap,

lead them burning green to drink
from the deep-violet jetting her breast.

We go where there is love,

to the river, on our knees beneath the sweet
water. I pull her under four times,

       until we are rivered.
       We are rearranged.

I wash the silk and silt of her from my hands—:
now who I come to, I come clean to,

       I come good to.

Notes

From the Desire Field:

This poem is one in a series of "letter-poems" Ada Limón and I sent back and forth over the course of a year, in 2018.

The phrase "*verde que te quiero verde*" is taken from Federico García Lorca's "Romance Sonámbulo," which is also referenced in the line "soy una sonámbula," sonámbula meaning sleepwalker.

Manhattan Is a Lenape Word:

This poem was written during a small micro-residency at the Ace Hotel New York, at the invitation and generosity of Alexander Chee. I was asked to stay a night in the hotel and write something.

The first line is in conversation with Anne Sexton's poem "The Truth the Dead Know," in which she wrote, "It is June. I am tired of being brave."

The "glittering world" is one way our Mojave creation story has been translated, since the earth was still wet, so rocks and dirt gleamed. It is also the often-used translation of the Diné origin story, and a few other Indigenous stories I have been told.

American Arithmetic:

These statistics are from Department of Justice reports. The reports shift from year to year, though the numbers stay low in regard to Indigenous population and rise in regard to violences our Indigenous peoples suffer. It is possible that other reports will yield different numbers, or that applying different configurations or equations to these statistics will produce different results. These are the numbers and statistics I worked with when I wrote the poem.

The line "Police kill Native Americans more than any other race" is based on statistics per capita, as the poem goes on to state in following lines. This poem was written in acknowledgment of, solidarity with, and in conversation with the police violence perpetrated against all black and brown peoples in the United States.

Skin-Light:

This poem is written in celebration of the original ball games and ball courts in what is now South and North America. These games were early versions of basketball and fútbol. Teotlachco was an important ball court, used for game and ceremony.

Asterion's Lament:

This poem references Jorge Luis Borges's "House of Asterion" and Robert Fagles's translation of *The Odyssey*, which states that Theseus "had no joy of her," in reference to Ariadne. Ariadne gave Theseus these instructions for moving through the labyrinth: "Go forward always down. . . ."

Like Church:

The line "*Sometimes I feel fast. Sometimes I am so slow*" is nodding to Nice & Smooth's song "Sometimes I Rhyme Slow." Their lyrics are "Sometimes I rhyme slow sometimes I rhyme quick."

The line "*What's in your love's eyes?*" is a line by Etel Adnan.

The line "If we didn't exist, it wouldn't be long before they had to invent us" is inspired by Hortense Spillers's *Mama's Baby, Papa's Maybe: An American Grammar Book*. Her original line is an epigraph for this book.

Wolf OR-7:

This poem was built as I watched a few different websites devoted to recording the movements of the wolf named OR-7.

Ink-Light:

The phrase "I touch her with the eyes of my skin" is taken from Finnish architect Juhani Pallasmaa's work titled *The Eyes of the Skin*.

The italicized ingredients listed in the third stanza are taken from an old recipe for ink.

Ode to the Beloved's Hips:

The line "*I wanna rock, I-I wanna rock, I-I wanna rock right now*" is from Rob Base and DJ EZ Rock's song "It Takes Two."

The orchard of Alcinous is referenced as described in *The Odyssey*. It was Odysseus's last stop before returning home.

The final stanza is about Spanish bullfighter Manuel Laureano Rodríguez Sánchez, known as Manolete, who Lorca wrote about in several poems. He died in his final season of bullfighting. As he killed the Miura bull named Islero, the bull gored him.

That Which Cannot Be Stilled:

This poem is part of the series written with Ada Limón. The phrase "*land and its moving*" is taken from the letter Ada wrote me, to which I was responding.

"*Do you feel a sense of doom?*" is a question a doctor asked me when I went to the emergency room for an anxiety attack.

"It's true that life can be anything, but certain things / definitely aren't it" are lines by John Ashbery in his poem "Life Is a Dream."

"*Beloved Occupier*" is a term a Palestinian student used to address Israel in a poem he wrote and read to us at Al-Quds Bard College of Arts and Sciences in East Jerusalem, West Bank, where I was a guest of the Palestinian Literary Festival. He isn't named here for his own safety.

"*Stiff Green Gallop*" is from the Doors' song "Horse Latitudes."

exhibits from *The American Water Museum*:

This space has been on my mind since I first read Luis Alberto Urrea's *The Water Museum*. The poem is not in conversation with Luis's book directly, but the book's title made a water museum a real space in my wonders. This poem is a small part of how the American Water Museum of my mind exists.

The phrase "*even a river will die of thirst*" is echoing the title of a collection of writings by Mahmoud Darwish: *A River Will Die of Thirst*.

Isn't the Air Also a Body, Moving?:

This is another poem in reply to Ada Limón's letter-poems. There is a nod to Robert Creeley at the end, since Ada had brought him into our conversation. In his poem "Song," he opens and ends the poem with the lines, "What I took in my hand / grew in weight," and "What / I took in my hand / grows in weight." I wasn't thinking of his poem when I read Ada's letter, but after going back through the poems, I believe this line must have come from Creeley, or for him.

If I Should Come Upon Your House Lonely in the West Texas Desert:

Language in this poem has leaped from "The Three Little Bears," which I was remixing for my niece over the phone before I sat down to write this poem. In terms of the oral story, these are some of the phrases that rose up from my telling: "Just right," which is what the narrator says each time Goldilocks finds something that suits her, and "eat it all up," which is what she did to the baby bear's porridge, and "break all your chairs to pieces," since she broke baby bear's chair. Finally, "And here I still am," which is a leap from "And here she still is," which is how I tell the moment when they found her in baby bear's bed. This is also a Marfa poem.

Grief Work:

Auxocromo and Cromóforo are in reference to a letter Frida Kahlo wrote to Diego Rivera: "Tu te llamarás AUXOCROMO el que capta el color. Yo CROMOFORO – la que da el color." Or, as translated: "You could be called Auxocromo—the one who takes color. I Cromoforo—the one who gives color."

Acknowledgments

Gracias to the interlocutors, instigators, storytellers, wonderers, lovers and lovers of languages, amig@s y familia, who are part of my image-scape, language-scape, and heart-scape.

Gracias to Jeff Shotts and the Graywolf team for inviting me into your family, and for your intentionality and care.

Gracias to the following journals, spaces, and editors who held these poems in their earliest versions and publics: *The Academy of American Poets' Poem-a-Day*, *The Believer*, *BOMB*, *Boston Review*, *BuzzFeed*, *Connotations Press* and *A Poetry Congeries*, *Drunken Boat*, *Freeman's*, *Indian Country Today*, *The Kenyon Review*, *Lenny Letter*, *Literary Hub*, *Narrative Magazine*, *New Poets of Native Nations*, *The New Republic*, *The New Yorker*, *Orion*, *The Paris-American*, *PEN America*, *Poetry*, *Prairie Schooner*, *Southern Humanities Review*, *Spillway Journal*, *Tales of Two Americas: Stories of Inequality in a Divided Nation*, and *thethepoetry.com*.

Gracias to the following foundations and persons who have opened their doors and imaginations, collaborating with me in energy and wonder as I wandered toward many of these poems: Jen Benka and all the good heart and mind work she does for poetry; Alex Dimitrov, Matthew Shinoda, and Samiya Bashir who placed some of these poems in the Academy of American Poets' Poem-a-Day; Saeed Jones at BuzzFeed News, Carin Kuoni of Vera List Center; and to Kwame Dawes for always pushing and sparking and helping me bring the basketball to the page. Gracias a la maestra Elizabeth Alexander who has changed the landscape of love, intellect, and imagination for all of us, on and off the page. Gracias to Michael Wiegers and Copper Canyon for your support.

Gracias to Patrick Lannan, Martha Jessup, Jo Chapman, and the Lannan Foundation—you have made so much poetry and language possible for me, including this book.

Gracias to the following people and spaces where I have been invited, held, supported, and inspired: Tracy K. Smith and Susan Wheeler at Princeton

University's Lewis Center for the Arts Hodder Fellowship; Dana Prescott and Civitella Ranieri Foundation; Deana Haggag and the United States Artists Foundation; Native Arts and Cultures Foundation; Jessica Rankin and Denniston Hill; Tyler Meier and the University of Arizona Poetry Center; Alexander Chee and the Ace Hotel New York Dear Reader Residency; The MacArthur Foundation; the Rupert Residency Program; the College at Arizona State University including my colleagues in Creative Writing and Jeffery Cohen, Krista Ratcliffe, Mark Searle, and President Michael Crowe.

Gracias to the numerous students, poets, writers, communities, schools, organizations, and universities who invited me into your spaces and allowed me to wonder, and where I read many of these works first, and where I was fed by your imaginations and kindnesses. Gracias to Hannah Ensor and Eloisa Amezcua for your friendship, support, and work. Gracias to Christine Sandoval for asking me to think alongside you about water. Gracias to Ana Maria Alvarez y Contra-Tiempo, Liz Lerman, CALA Alliance and the Bi-National Arts Residency for dancing toward the water with me. Gracias a Jehan Bseiso, Omar Robert Hamilton, Nathalie Handal, Sharif Kouddous, and Ahdaf Soueif, and the Palestinian Festival of Literature family—your work makes us all more possible. Gracias to the students from Al-Quds Bard and Hebron University for sharing your stories, dreams, and rigorous imaginations with me.

Gracias a mis herman@s y mi equipo, Solmaz Sharif, Roger Reeves, and Rickey Laurentiis. You three are my trinity—how lucky to have found you through poetry, and then to have you all become so much more than poetry to me. Gracias to Rachel Eliza Griffiths, Ada Limón, Kamilah Aisha Moon, and Brenda Shaughnessy—mis hermanas y mis guerreras en poesía. Gracias to Christian Campbell, my brother in heart, imagination, and power. Gracias to Fady Joudah who offered me love, patience, and care—I would not be where I am in this day without the friendship and strength you showed me. Gracias to Mary Szybist for wondering alongside me and toward me. Mil gracias y amor a Monique Cover, who first gave me the gift of poetry.

Gracias to Joy Harjo, Deborah Miranda, Heid E. Erdrich, Louise Erdrich, Kim Blaser, Ofelia Zepeda, Karen Wood, LeAnne Howe, and the many

Native women who have made and continue to make poetry a place where we can exist, and who have become my Elders and family.

Gracias to my mentor and friend Dr. Bryan Brayboy who offers me and so many other Native women more than he will ever know of our imagination and futurity—I am lucky for you.

Gracias a mi familia, Bernadette, Richard, Richie, Sis, John, Desirae, Gabriella, Belarmino, Sarah, Valentin, Serena, Franki, David, Liv, and also to my Aunt Patsy.

Gracias to the storytellers before me, whose energies and languages I carry in me. Inyech 'asumach 'ahota. Ojalá.

Gracias a Saretta, mi media naranja, mi mañana. "Sé que cuando te llame / entre todas las gentes / del mundo, / sólo tú serás tú."—Pedro Salinas.

Gracias a ti, Reader, for entering these poems and making them, and the persons and stories living in them, including you and me, always possible.

Dedication

Toward the missing and murdered Indigenous and Native women, girls, trans women, nonbinary and two spirit people in our families, communities, and across the Americas and other occupied lands—in thinking of the touch and tenderness you deserve;

toward my mother, who generously imagined and taught me a way of love along which I and my beloveds can be the most possible;

toward our many bodies of flesh, language, land, and water;

toward all we have been born for, and carry, and have yet to become of love.

NATALIE DIAZ was born and raised in the Fort Mojave Indian Village in Needles, California, on the banks of the Colorado River. She is Mojave and an enrolled member of the Gila River Indian Tribe. Her first poetry collection, *When My Brother Was an Aztec*, won an American Book Award. She is a 2018 MacArthur Fellow, as well as a Lannan Literary Fellow and a Native Arts and Cultures Foundation Artist Fellow. She was awarded the Holmes National Poetry Prize and a Hodder Fellowship from Princeton University. She is a member of the Board of Trustees for the United States Artists, where she is an alumna of the Ford Fellowship. Diaz is the Maxine and Jonathan Marshall Chair in Modern and Contemporary Poetry at Arizona State University.

The text of *Postcolonial Love Poem* is set in Minion Pro.
Book design by Rachel Holscher.
Composition by Bookmobile Design & Digital Publisher Services,
Minneapolis, Minnesota.
Manufactured by Versa Press on acid-free,
30 percent postconsumer wastepaper.